Mother Fur

Nadia Arioli

Fernwood
PRESS

Mother Fur
©2025 by Nadia Arioli

Fernwood Press
Newberg, Oregon
www.fernwoodpress.com

All rights reserved. No part may be reproduced
for any commercial purpose by any method without
permission in writing from the copyright holder.

Printed in the United States of America

Cover and page design: Mareesa Fawver Moss
Cover image: Mariusz Słoński - https://unsplash.com/@maledobro

ISBN 978-1-59498-181-4

For Samuel and Frances

*Samuel, I wrote this for you, but now it is for you both.
Frances, the next book will be the other way around.*

"It is not enough to bear," writes Nadia Arioli; "one must erase all evidence of having done so." This book sheds light on what it costs to bring another person into being, and stands as a bold refusal to hide that cost. In deeply embodied writing, Arioli pits archetype against reality in order to illuminate the human and profoundly *animal* experience of motherhood. Arioli's gift for word-on-word poetic friction builds a devastating heat that makes honesty inescapable. This writing demands we understand the exhaustion, tenderness, pain, and absurdity of birth and motherhood and the fact that each of us owes our existence to "life pulled from a wound."

—LISA HUFFAKER
teaching artist in residence for the Writer's Garret

Nadia Arioli's *Mother Fur* is that rare commonality that is both an interrogation of crowded stillness and a confessional written in the ghost dark of movingly lonely observation. Spiritually tactile and physically worshipful of the exhaustion that invents fatigue, it is a verse that musics itself beyond the chorus of admittance and into the recalled invitation of a witness that acts as the inner life of the photo. A work of protection and parenthetical braveries, it is full of a draining care specific enough to parent emptiness in all its bullied and stray forms.

—BARTON SMOCK,
author of *Wasp, Gasp*

To enter the gorgeous music of *Mother Fur* is to become one with lyrics that sing of a new birth, these songs resonating with the beautiful mystery of the rebirthing moments within our lives. A triumph of compassion and lyricism, *Mother Fur* unveils the growing truths that await us all.

—DWAINE RIEVES,
author of *When the Eye Forms* and *Shirtless Men Drink Free*

Nadia Arioli's *Mother Fur* is a wonder that begins and ends with tenderness—a new mother teaching her "son / to use / dandelions / instead of / flame," a new mother coaxing a banished family cat into her lap to be loved. But *Mother Fur* is no Mary Cassatt painting of early motherhood, all "pink and green… a sacred circus." It is instead a hardscrabble landscape— one of loss, the complexities of familial bonds, and the search for identity, all centered in the unlikely mythic figure of Grendel's mother. Grendel's mother, who lives and breathes and struggles in a sequence of fifteen astonishing poems that comprise *Mother Fur*'s fearless animal middle. Grendel's mother considers, yes, many things from her inimitable vantage point, even the need for "convalescing"—which she boards a Greyhound bus to accomplish. What a ride.

—Robin Turner,
author of *bindweed & crow poison*

Table of Contents

I. 9
   In Defense of Gentleness 10
   Snapshots for My Family 11
   Painting by Mary Cassatt 13
   Hole Shapes 14
   Watching Perry Mason with
      a Mouth Full of Vomit 16
   Red Sea Whale 18
   Teaching My Son Poetry 20

II. 21
   Grendel's Mother Considers Wells Beach, Maine 22
   Grendel's Mother Considers the Surinam Toad 23
   Grendel's Mother Considers Ortolans 24
   Grendel's Mother Considers Therapy 25
   Grendel's Mother Considers the Sphinx Moth 29
   Grendel's Mother Considers Pigs 31
   Grendel's Mother Considers
      the Bones You Cannot Touch 32
   Grendel's Mother Considers Ants 33

Grendel's Mother Considers the Giraffes 34
Grendel's Mother Considers Convalescing 35
Grendel's Mother Considers
   the Pink Fairy Armadillo 37
Grendel's Mother Considers Eve 38
Grendel's Mother Considers Vinegar 39
Grendel's Mother Considers Christ the Starfish 40
Grendel's Mother Considers the Sea Turtles 41

III. 43
   (Hair / Loss) 44

Notes on Poems 79
Acknowledgments 81
Title Index 83
First Line Index 85

I.

In Defense of Gentleness

I teach
my son
to use
dandelions
instead of
flame.

Snapshots for My Family

I am all camera—I
    have no knowledge of my inner workings.
Each contraction is a hanging,
    like spools of film catching wrong.
The doctors decide to cut me open—
    springing the fat roll of you out,
perfect canister of blood and organs.
    Mine but not mine. The doctors slice a straight line,
finding a brand-new flap, and out you snap,
    all vowels, a screech of light.

I, camera, try to document with
    my drug-addled, pain-addled mind,
        saying, *You must remember*
all this as it happens. The drive
over for what was planned, the
    induced labor that almost is
        the death of you. On the way,
we listen to Django Reinhardt,
we get soggy sandwiches.
    Turkey and avocado on whole wheat.

    My belly became telescopic with you,
    reaching for the heavens,
        or, more accurately, outwards in red lines
        like the first camera. A bloated box
            the size of god, surrounded by men in coats.
        One man hangs on the edge of the aperture
    like an inverse bat. *Photograph of the First*
    Camera Being Built, the caption says.
O historic occasion! O unity of makers!

But then who or what took the photo? A time-traveler?
   (When they took your first ultrasound, the doctor
saw cysts and untamed uterine growth, said conception
     would be difficult, but I already had.)
Was it mirrors displayed elaborately that allowed
              the camera to take a photo of itself?
(You are a miracle of light.) Or was the photo
     a staged recreation? (I am trying to write the story of you.)
   Now I know it was you, life pulled from a wound,
you, Sam, who saw me being made.

Painting by Mary Cassatt

It's okay to be tender. Here,
light creates itself, has always
been creating itself. The belly
of the child becomes marble, a plump pillar.
A woman with dark hair fuses her forehead
with her child's, her dress a pink
and green linen tent. A sacred circus.
The world around them melts into
meadows of dressers and flooring.
That child is going to get so clean.

When the poet was a child,
they cared only for the beauty of mind,
a world where there is nothing to touch,
nothing to do the touching,
not even the light. Sage, Kahlo, Oppenheim.
Softness of form, not body,
because tenderness was never safe.
The poet's mother accused:
*Why can't you just love paintings
that are nice, like* The Child's Bath?
The poet vowed to always hate Cassatt.

In the museum, a tired mother lifts
her fussing child from his stroller by his armpits.
He swings like an acrobat. She reaches into her
breast pocket on her flannel shirt and pulls
out a pacifier with a magician's flourish.
The baby gulps on it for a second and then
tries desperately to put it in his mother's
mouth and then her eye. She laughs too
loudly for a gallery and scrunches up her face.
The baby giggles until he doesn't at her refusal.
We have always given each other unwelcome gifts.

Hole Shapes

Wet webs blanket the grass in mornings
in Scotland and North America. Congealed
dew. Plasticine rain. No scientists can
agree on the composition. It contains no DNA
or known origin. Nature writers of old
called it *star jelly*, with the thought
shooting stars had a byproduct. No—not
byproduct, remnant, a memory before
the stars sped on. A hearty slime painting
the planet below. We know now
what is too distant, what burns too much
up, but we're still no closer to an answer
than that old story.

In 1996, in Arizona, cars speed on by
suburban intersections, bent poles
like arthritis where stop signs should be.
Not natural causes but yanked by human hands.
I, a child, wanting to know
the comings and goings of all things,
asked my mother as she was driving
who would do such a thing—
make a wound metallic where order should be.
And my mother said that people take,
you know, what isn't theirs to take,
because they don't need it.
They think, *Well, I've already stopped,
I don't need this anymore.* So they
get out of their cars and just take the sign.
I harumphed, too young to need a story.

There are many reasons to feign delicacy.
One is to turn fault lines into jokes.
One is to see how fluid catches light
and call it from the stars.
One is to account for the place a stone is
instead of a mother's love.

Watching Perry Mason with
a Mouth Full of Vomit

We call my grandmother as she is dying,
long distance, my sister and I. What is
there to say? It's been a decade, we're sorry

you're dying, remember us? Even
though I am on my cell phone, I am picturing
cords spanning continents, curling

like umbilicals, like ribbons
on a welcome gift, like sashes
on a casket. I want to tell my grandmother

I, too, have tether now,
there is a fourth, but my body
is like the hospital my grandmother
is at: not a place for getting stronger,

just where the fragile go to die,
and my sister is on the phone too, and I
don't want to be a further disappointment.
So my sister and I say, *We love you, we're here.*

My grandmother croaks, *I don't feel so good*,
and the rest is all vowels, because she can
no longer swallow. Choking, gurgling,
as if her mouth is the deepest cave.

I tell her that we can't understand,
the connection is static (a white lie)
but I'm glad we got through. She dies

the next day. I take three Tums
instead of two, the heartburn tearing
harder in my chest. Mourning sickness.

I turn on Perry Mason, even though
that channel has tons of static. I watch
what could be any episode with a mouth full of vomit.

Because Perry always knows what to say,
so articulate, so calm, perfect mid-Atlantic.
The truth will out, justice will be served.

Death is always sudden, even sexy.
Perry gets the last word in before the credits roll.
And everything, everything is tied up nicely with a bow.

Red Sea Whale

My son has a mouth
like the Red Sea, parting

in two perfect halves, the gums
sprays of spit over them.

Oooh ooh ooh, he cries,
teething. A small nub on

the lower left, white, arching,
a whale. I had wondered

as a child about the marine
life when God commanded Moses

to part the sea. Small of the shallows,
big of the deeps, all made vertical,

a parfait of salt and wild. I thought
this the better sort of love

than what God showed Moses.
And why shouldn't God have a special fondness

for whales? Both ponderous and just
under the surface of things? The

weightlessness of not being given
a choice, no burning bush, no being

left outside the promised land.
Only up, up, up, toward the divine,

holy tooth, bursting through skin.
My son is growing out not up, and

his Red Sea has wails of a different
sort. I hold him until he sleeps.

There is no way to explain God to him,
why his bones must break through his own body.

And would I, if I could? I've spent too
much time in the deep. I had forgotten

until now what happens
when God says, *Up, up, up.*

Teaching My Son Poetry

Kitten, I read to my son
from a touch-and-feel book,
Meow! Meow! and I show
him the picture of orange stripes
with yarn. It looks like our cat
but smaller and more wide-eyed.
Puppy, I read next, Woof! Woof!
and I let him touch where the picture
gives way to soft, white fluff
like a forest emptying to a meadow.
Tiger cub, licking his nose!
Baby chimpanzee. Ooh-ooh. Aah-aah.
Starfish. Five long arms.
Butterfly, flutter, flutter, flutter.

Soon, I will give him other tools
for knowing the world.
Odometers for how far he's been,
spectrometers for when
light is only wave,
cyanometers for the blueness of the sky.

For now, I lay my son in his crib.
He's almost asleep, and I've
leaked through my shirt again.
I dig through his crate of soft toys
—everything is soft in babyland—
and put his small elephant on his chest.
The mother elephant it came with
feels too heavy. I make the baby elephant
nuzzle my son's face with its snout.
Starfish, I say, five long arms.

II.

Grendel's Mother Considers Wells Beach, Maine

Imagine that, not wanting or needing a name. Each
droplet in the ocean cannot be summoned
but moves as one body does. Grendel's mother
floats, her girth turned to blubber to be carried.
She learned how to swim in the forest, in whirlpools
of leaf-rot and dirt. It's lighter out here, in the Atlantic,
drowsy and empty, sunbaked belly, sand-baked paws.

No one seems to notice her, the beachgoers all
one plant with umbrella blooms. So,
Grendel's mother swims by the beach, unafraid of
being hunted but afraid to really drift out there,
afraid to truly become less / more. She is half-dissolved now, like
the moonlight on water—there but not.

She considers that the other swimmers don't go full
liquid either. A human mother in her one size
too small two-piece dives headfirst
into the waves, mouth open for salt, seaweed,
and wild. Grendel's mother surmises the swimmer
is tired of filling herself with sweet things and takes
in what she can get. And yet, she too, doesn't give.
The human mother looks over her shoulder at her family
on the beach, pale husband, small child eating sand. Imagine
    that,
though, still having an anchor that's actual, thinks Grendel's
    mother,
imagine having someone calling you from the shore.
Imagine a reason to stay.

Grendel's Mother Considers the Surinam Toad

Your brats are bursting,   big with love,
hatching through honeycomb,   heavy hearts.
You are the constant courier.   They come out complete
like hoped-for homunculi.   I happened there when
the miracle in murk   made its mark
on my eyes.   O overflow
of self, no sire   of slime. You make lonesomeness
a complete circle.   Your kind cannot
comprehend helplessness.   Which were hewn
as daughters, with dimples,   dappled all the way down?
No red, no remove,   raw seedlings
You perfect creature,   you microcosm of carbuncular life.
And departure does go   in dozens then done
Your back says it's done   and then it's done
Closure is not one crack.   My child is gone.
Trypophobia is fear   of fauna unfathomable.
Deemed Delphic,   dormant venom.
In this hole, an asp,   in this nest, wasps.
One night-furred in a nest.   I could never fear you,
I love you. I love you,   I love you, I love you.

Grendel's Mother Considers Ortolans

How do you manage it—slow
death like adoration, my buntings,
my bloated flaps? In darkness,
they fed you until you almost
popped because that is what we do
when we can't see: Consume until
we burst, turning our bodies as large
as houses to do what houses do,
body a container for fear. How
was the anointing, did it feel
like desire transfigured into
sacrament, Armagnac unction and poison,
poison in little lungs that sung
with their cousins in coal mines?

And then, how was the final
birth in reverse, feet first,
although I suppose you came from egg
not womb. In went your twiggy feet,
in went your branchy legs.
Guts in a big bite like feathered ravioli.

                              (My similes are full of holes,
      but so are the nets they used to catch you, my ortolans.)

When I go it won't be like this—
It won't be disgusting and illegal and tender.
Is it so wrong to desire this? Beowulf,
I know it is useless, but I am asking:
Do it as planning, do it as treat.
Do it while hiding from God.

Grendel's Mother Considers Therapy

but not as an alternative to revenge. More of a *yes
and*, like you see in improv troupes, but this is no laughing
   matter.
She gets jittery at the thought of it, like someone who's had
   too much
espresso, including the bathroom aspect of that. Grendel's
   mother
considers therapy. Her insurance will pay for it, it would seem.
Or part of it, or sometimes there's a co-pay and sometimes
   there isn't.
Grendel's mother isn't too sure. She's been distracted of late,
   which is
something therapy could probably help her with. Grendel's
   mother
seeks validation, which, wow, embarrassing, but she wants
   permission
to own her grief. Permission—what a laugh. Grendel's mother
   doesn't knock.

Grendel's mother considers the logistics, the travel time. She
   doesn't
have pockets to put the insurance card and paper check and so
   forth in.
She doesn't drive a car and can't seem to make heads or tails of
   the bus schedule.
She used to be about to but can't anymore. Also, she's a
   monster.
She can hardly amble down Main Street without catching
a scream or two. And most of the time finding a therapist is a
   whole thing
and involves making phone calls and even—god forbid!—
   leaving a voicemail.

Why do they make it so complicated? Grendel's mother rages.
    Therapy
is for people who are in a state such that they cannot do
    complex tasks, so why not
make it as complicated as possible? Why the hell not? The
    barriers are bigger than walls.
And Grendel's mother remembers all the complex things she
    used to do—chewing
bones into paste and baby-birding it into Grendel's maw.
    Building camouflage
for the front of her cave when he was born out of twigs and
    leaves held
together with mud and intention. Timing the raids just right
    until
Grendel got the hang of it until he didn't.

Grendel's mother imagines making a day of it, going to
    therapy. It's only
in the next town, but errands have a way of taking over the
    whole day
even if it's really just an hour or two. Maybe she could stop and
    get coffee
on the way or stop at the picnic tables on the way back for
    lunch or even
just a smoke. Therapy makes one want cigarettes, even if you've
    quit, so much
breathing in yourself, your scent, your mistakes, that it feels
    good
to breath in something else, anything else, even poison, even
    cancer,
that isn't just your own bullshit.

Grendel's mother imagines that in the past she went to therapy, right
after Grendel was born, say, that's when she did it. She went, drove herself
because she had a car in those days. The therapist's office is nice but bland. There's a
certain decorating style to therapist's offices, isn't there? It's trying very
hard to not be any one thing. Her and her therapist have a good rapport.
She tells her therapist of her intense need to be desired but not desired, to be
touched but not touched, and how the hormones are making her a monster. She wails,
clutching tissues in her right claw, she doesn't even know who she is anymore,
between the feedings and the wiping and the late nights, who is she anymore. Her body
is pudgy around the middle, and no one wants to see her in a swimsuit anymore,
not that they really did in the first place. And who the fuck,
who the fuck does she think she is seeking validation through men,
the men, the men, always the men with them looking at her before they
saw prey, saw threat, saw target.

Grendel's mother considers leaving an audience for grief and decides she hates the thought.
Grief is valid, she thinks, unknown grief is valid. Leave no witnesses. Leave no

one to hear wails. You don't need a confessor to absolve you,
   you don't need a stranger
scribbling in a notebook. You don't need a written record
   shoved and forgotten
in a drawer. You were born alone. You don't remember it, but
   you are sure.
Your mother whelped you out, wet ball of fur, helpless and
   disgusting. For a time,
you weren't alone, second self, guiding star. Then you were
   alone again,
and it was worse, somehow. No matter. No matter the gaps
in your teeth. No matter that your cries are different—hollow
like caves, hollow like empty nests, hollow like bullets.
You just need your claws. You can write the whole thing in red.

Grendel's Mother Considers the Sphinx Moth

I am trying to find a story in which an animal is written about fairly.

In Edgar Allan Poe's short story *The Sphinx*, the narrator is quarantined with his friend to try to weather a plague. It sounds familiar because it is. Death is ravaging the countryside, word arrives that their friends are dead. No longer just a fact, death is a force that's hard to explain but nonetheless true, like love, magnets, and God.

In this state, the narrator looks out of the window and sees a foul beast charging down the hillside, crushing the landscape with its terrible legs. The twist, of course—and these things always have a twist—is that the beast is merely a sphinx moth on a tendril in front of the window. It was a trick of forced perspective, like a photo your uncle might take of you holding up the Tower of Pisa.

The ending is that the beast isn't real, and all is well. Except, not really, because the terror at such a monster was real, the feeling of dread and like you're losing your mind are real. The lesson is, don't let fear get the better of you. The lesson is, sometimes scary things are small, like a drop of blood carrying a plague, like a baby.

Several times a year, the female sphinx moth lays eggs, typically in a clutch, all on the same flower. Depending on the subspecies, the eggs take between three and twenty-one days to hatch. Like all butterflies and moths, the young are born as caterpillars, usually with five pairs of prolegs. Sometimes, a subspecies may have a horn on the end, which is why a sphinx moth can be known as a horned caterpillar.

(Strange that an infant can be so different than the parent. A wonder the moths can reproduce at all.)

(When he was born, I looked in his eyes and saw myself.)

The young hold themselves in a push-up-like pose and head facing forward, like a sphinx at the great pyramid of Giza.

So, it's not about riddles. Tell me: What is bigger when it's far away?

The young are camouflaged. To have quiet children who are nothing like you.

Then the caterpillars do what caterpillars do, namely transform into moths, and that is beautiful and profound and not at all like a beast-mother terrorizing down a hill. The imaginal cells turn to goo, and the full moth emerges. The mothers are gone by that point, but the cells know—hardcoded into DNA.

They live lives that have nothing to do with us, with me, monster in red and fur, nor you, reader.

How close do you think you can get to me? Can you creep in deerskin boots to where I lay? Am I smaller close up or far away? How is it that I always picture Grendel as a baby when he was slaughtered, and not a full-grown beast, six legs wriggling?

Grendel's Mother Considers Pigs

O small beast with little hooves,
they've watched you grow bloatedly.
Wild thing they tamed then denigrated
for being caged, your pink anatomy
is not like mine nor your pink jailers.
You look at the muck they stuck you in,
and snuffle around for grubs. Your neck
is stuck like that, from what I've surmised,
unable to see the stars.
Once, I tried to approach, hold
you in my fur arms, as if you
were my children, toothy animals,
children of Cain. (This was before
he was born.) But you sensed my coming,
and the squealing was unbearable.
I slunk away.

I had a dream, after Grendel.
We were both children again
and decided to get a pet, and
one morning, we woke up, came
downstairs, and in the middle of the living room
were three holes, black and round like puddles.
I scooped one into my arms, held it
there to my chest. The hole
was the size of a piglet.
I took it outside and tilted it
up toward the stars as dawn
was poking its snout through the clouds.
In my arms, squealing.

Grendel's Mother Considers the Bones You Cannot Touch

                in the room   of given   light
in the museum   where children go,
        each in a line   of linked bones
     there is a colossus   indelible
more real than dragons   or other monsters
          larger too   the bones are for looking
but not touching.   never
touching
remote as any icon-beast made saint
            beast made sacred   and like plovers
and infants   all terrible mouth.

Grendel's Mother Considers Ants

The way to carry is to care.
You would have taken the arm as well,
a hundred thousand of you.
You have to be strong to be small.
O ants, can you lift my prayer?

Grendel's Mother Considers the Giraffes

Nobody knows how you do it.　　　Other beasts
have mewls and croaks and roars.　　But you,
you have your vast silence　　and eyes big like a baby's
stares and ways scientists cannot uncover.　　After
all that, while they were writing　　a book about me,
I shook myself down south　　and stalked a herd.
I saw an alphabet in neck.　　*I am running*,
I am running, said one neck,　　and the other necks said *I too*.
The giraffes made *n*'s when they bent down　　to their small ones—
Nothing will ever hurt you.　　And the giraffes could spell
out more things as a family—　　two kissing at the ground for
more more, together we are more.　　And only together
could they make *L*'s.　　They spelled this shape when nursing.
The mother the stem, calf the arm.　　The *L* was for loss,
there at the beginning,　　even before the hole.
L for loss, slurp slurp, *L* for loss.　　It has already begun.

Grendel's Mother Considers Convalescing

in a sanatorium or a jail cell. It doesn't much matter which. But,
   for now, she'll settle for a Greyhound. The grosser the better. So,
   Grendel's mother packs
her horrible suitcase with her horrible clothes after purchasing a
ticket online (everything is so convenient these days), taxies to
   the station
and gets on. The bus is stinky the way a hotel room is just-
   cleaned-with-too-many-chemicals
stinky, so you know it must have been nast. There is something
   soothing,
something soporific about that smell, Grendel's mother muses,
   and she is glad of it.

Grendel's mother considers convalescing but takes the bus
   instead. It's the best
she can do. She buys all the candy she has coins for at the
   vending machine at the terminal
and no one can stop her. On the bus, she sits near the back, a
   bad kid for life,
and hunkers down to watch the other passengers board. None
   look particularly
tasty, which is a good thing because Grendel's mother does not
   wish to make
a whole scene, and she has her candy anyways, Sour Patch Kids,
   off-brand grandma candy too,
those strawberry ones that taste like cough-drops in the red and
   green wrappers.

Grendel's mother considers convalescing, which none of the
   other passengers have considered.
They're going about their business, vaguely unaware that one is
   not human. They are

all the huddled masses, they are all the unwashed. Bus people.
   Grendel's mother
can consider herself better or worse than them but knows the
   truth—
it's all bus people on the bus. Grendel's mother looks out the
   window and sees
trash from bus people, fast-food places for bus people, every
   intersection is the same
in America, and she sees a lot of it. She eats her candy. She
   considers

convalescing. This is her convalescing because being a single
   mom is really, really hard.
She puts her feet up on her suitcase in front of her, and hums.
   Only one passenger
this whole trip has spoken to her, after a whole day together. A
   loud chewer
in a cowboy hat. *Where're ya headed?* he jaws. Grendel's mother
   looks out
right into the sun, sliding down, normally about the time she
   wakes up.
She answers slowly, quietly, careful not to show her teeth. *West,
   baby*,
says Grendel's mother, *I'm headed west.*

Grendel's Mother Considers the Pink Fairy Armadillo

Your armor is pathetic—O my sashimi, my sand-snake,
my burrow-bear. Nobody can save you—although
your peril is nuanced. Men only want what is dolphin,
squeaky, hairless, accessible hole, and you are the antithesis,
with your white bristles, lobster claws, and dorsal covering.
And yet, you are not altogether safe, for all your caution.
Destined for a life of doom in captivity. What is it
I can say to you, small knight, or are you monster
like me, all hard, all shard, all unknowable? Once,
I let you crawl on the tip of my maw, you small anomaly,
unafraid of me, with my snuffle-fur, my bad breath, the hole
where Grendel used to live. Can you tell me
of your secrets, in underground places? Can you
tell me how it feels when death works better than your armor?

Grendel's Mother Considers Eve

im sorry
i was looking
for lillith

Grendel's Mother Considers Vinegar

Fatherless as Grendel, the vinegar has not been generated,
just gestated. The mother was born as ugly as sin.
Ask me for octopus gut, for swamp belly, for thick
female mucus, and I will show you
the same for each, in fetching bottles,
innocuous and shelved. Do you feel it?
The shame and wonder of a generative force
but turned lurid by how wet it is? What could
be more wet and lurid than a mother? What could
be more wet and repulsive than a mother?
What could be more wet? I think
our purpose the same, vinegar and I.
We clean and clean with acid claw. We clean, so
they can gag at us behind bars. What
else will unsoil? What else will eat the dead? You need us
to keep your hands clean. This is the state of the world:
Gross paw, slime mother, sealed jar.
Everyone already knows evil has no father.

Grendel's Mother Considers Christ the Starfish

Celestial Star, yours is the same as of the sea.
Anguished Grendel. Nothing could be grafted
once ripped right off. I was robbed twice.
A perfect pair, like the pink starfish
I could have had. However, one would've been enough.
I posed Pieta, prostrate son in pouring arms,
Did you deign to understand? No divine light
for Grendel and I, no grace. How gut-stopping
when yours returned remarkable. Crucified arm
with hole but still attached. When he arrived
was that moment for you mercurial—the marble becoming
flesh, unfreezing once more? When a starfish is fractured,
from both edges can a new whole emerge.
Which Christ came back? Now as we converse, conversely
it occurs to me you're cursed too. Christ cast you off
twice, O Lady. Once to tomb, once to eternity
without you. I offer you now these starfish,
kissy fish, spiny fish, strange spawning spawn
for blue mantle. You can make as many as you like.

Grendel's Mother Considers the Sea Turtles

You are fast but frigid. You forget the sounds
of sinew and these rough sibilants,   shrieks and braying.
Fat like a full mouth,   your flippers make wet cradles
in the water when wading,   but without a shelter made.
Inquire of my cave   beneath your blue quarters;
I will teach you my tongue,   same tongue of my foremothers.
Cleft off-center,   as though cut by a stone,
badly. I know breaks from before,   the one I gave my belly,
not a caesura like the split   of sand from wave.
Consider that I cut him out,   executing with the old sword.
I hacked haphazardly,   that eager was I to meet him.
The cord we shared he choked on. At his conclusion, he coughed.
His rage was spent in red tide. It erased his body.
My name too is no more,   now synonymous with wind.

Your broods were barely   in your body before
whelping them out like waste: tooth-white for prey.
Clutch, they called yours,   but I did it countless times.
In my womb waiting,   then wending him through my maw
when his eyes emitted   unending dark.
Men knew my manglers   but not the gaps among them.
My cave contains dust,   what came of his corpse.
Lot's wife, I look back. I lament, but not a fool.
Monster or mother,   what does it make me?
Silence, I may as well say,   silence and claws.
Gentle giants,   you are girls of Abel.
Turtles, transporting the world, I tire of my tirade.
You keep compelling on,   I keen backwards.
In the end, we both emptied   our children to eternity.

III.

(Hair / Loss)

A strange man is at my house when it is not yet light. He is petting my medium-haired creamsicle cat and is calling him "babydoll." I trust him with my life. I'm in a bit of a daze and my ratty pajamas: too-big t-shirt and plaid pants. My husband and I are in the throes of moving across the country with our five-month-old son, house full of junk, and all the baggage that entails after living over a decade in Texas. Our complete, separate lives that then merged, our collective boxes in the garage.

The strange, bespeckled man and his hippy-haired wife are here to pick up the orange creamsicle along with our three other cats: a spoiled orange-striped tabby, a sensitive Thai, and a gray-striped cat with an amazingly huge ass.

We are paying an exorbitant fee for this. For the physical transportation, yes, but also the peace of mind that comes with leaving your pets in the hands of professionals. The odd little man and his wife move gracefully through our bare living room, grab the four large cages, load them into a van to the sounds of a full choir, and vacate.

\--

The medium-haired creamsicle cat and I are approximating the same haircut. Sort of a shag-type deal. For me, the idea was the hide the gray, and you can't dye your hair while pregnant. (Well, you can, but my son is a double-rainbow boy, so I exercised every known and unknown precaution.) Then my hair started falling out in clumps postpartum, which is another thing about giving birth nobody tells you about—along with the farting, lack of shitting, and hemorrhoids. And I didn't want to dye my hair and damage it further. So now my dark hair falls out, the creamsicle's hair falls out too, and we are both allover a mess and neurotic about things.

During pregnancy, my hair blossomed into a wholesomeness unforetold by my years of frizzy thin puffs. I had attempted straightness and attempted bouncing, beautiful curls, like dozens of perfect breasts, but always fell rather flat. "Thin," "greasy," and "frizzy" are not the adjectives one aims for on one's hair journey. At the very least, the adjectives could have behaved decently and sort of balanced each other out. Instead, no, what I had was a mess. But during pregnancy, the halo became holy. Thick, bouncing curls adorned my fattening face. Full, shiny. The adjectives you wanted for a terrific bob but it's really an overgrown pixie on a journey through mullet-hood. But my hair glory was short-lived and a few months after I gave birth, strands started coming out. I knew the good locks were temporary, but if you're wondering if I could cope, the answer to that is a resounding "no."

The creamsicle cat's fur came out too. This was likely due to stress. Moving and a new baby can be hard on a fussy feline. Even before the little man showed up, the cats had to deal with all of our possessions going into boxes, the boxes being everywhere, and general chaos that comes with staging a fixer-upper of a '70s house to sell it while still living in it.

It would have been fine if fur were the only thing that came out of the creamsicle cat. But in the months leading up to the baby's arrival, the cat had taking to pissing and shitting in the dining room. It's as disgusting as it sounds. Every morning our noses would be greeted by an assault on the senses. Turds and puddles. We took the cat to the vet, of course—twice, actually, and the conclusion was the same both times: the issue was psychological. He would poop and pee because he was being attacked and bullied by the other three cats.

Here I could get defensive about having four male, unrelated cats. I could tell you about how I started off with one, the spoiled ginger tabby, whom I cherish overmuch because he belonged to a friend who passed, and my husband started off with two, the Thai and the creamsicle, who used to love each other but now would like nothing more than to devour each other, for reasons lost on us, and how the striped gray cat is because it was a pandemic and I was trying to process my second miscarriage. Or I could tell you that they all got along well, really well—until they didn't. The stress of a baby, of packing, was too much for their delicate sensibilities. But it doesn't really matter. You can think we're out of our minds or understand how such a thing could happen.

When the bullying started, we tried everything. Separation, which wasn't practical for the layout of a single-story, shotgun house, with an un-air-conditioned garage in Texas summer. Positive reinforcement, negative reinforcement. Sprays, plug-ins, all of it. We kept saying maybe it'll get better once we move, with a bigger house, and a house that doesn't smell like the previous owner's pets. Maybe getting out of Texas will solve all of our problems.

--

A problem I try to work out has to do with containers and language. For moving across the country, all our belongings go into shipping pods—called PODS—and then the PODS are moved via truck and arrive a week or so after we do in New England. Everything gets moved along as it should and is kept safe.

That's the idea anyway. We all know things will get damaged no matter how much we wrap and stack well. The legs of the yellow couch snap off, and the couch goes into the garage for fixing later. My husband says he thinks he can fix it—reach inside it and rehammer a board and then re-screw on the legs. I feel like I should care. The couch is newish, and it's pretty, and I do like it. I picked it out myself. But after everything, the stress of owning things in motion, I don't have any real feelings toward the couch one way or another.

There isn't really language to describe feeling not at home in a body that changed. There's not really language for not having a proper home for your skeleton while not at home. The closest word is *uncanny*.

I wanted words like efficient pods when I was a child and now that desire is returning. I used to stick things in parentheses. So instead of writing "I love you," I would write "(I love you.)" that way it wouldn't get hurt. It would be my little house that moved with me.

But that's silly and feels like a game. I'm a parent now and should not be playing games.

--

Once we're more settled in, I get a routine going. I try to listen more to the natural rhythms of the house and the people in it. I used to be rigorous always, with my alarms and schedules and lists. Most days sort of look the same now, but there's a comfort in that. After the boxes are moved into the house and the PODS are taken away (but we're nowhere near moved in yet) the days go into quiet patterns almost without my say so.

The baby wakes up around five to nurse. I usually can convince him to go back to bed after, and we wake up for real around eight-ish. I pet the kitties after my husband feeds them. We're keeping the creamsicle separate for now (long story) and it seems to be working, but it is an undertaking. We don't do things in the same order every day, but, generally, we play on the floor with Panda and ball and rattle. Then I read him a story. Then it's nap time for baby and I work on my lit mag (reading submissions, upload to the website, social media, typesetting, Patreon—this'll lessen once I get caught up). Then it's more nursing and rolling and a tour of the house with light switches and mirrors. Baby likes looking at himself in the mirror. If the weather is nice, which is hit-or-miss late fall, we walk. If not, just I go and my husband watches baby if his work-from-home schedule allows. Then more nursing. Then it's time for another nap and I do my art stuff like draw a picture, work on my poem or essay, and read a book about craft. Probably it's nursing time again. Then it's time for cleaning and unpacking and moving boxes around, if my in-laws can watch the baby or my husband can after his work. Somewhere in there, food happens. Then maybe a show if the baby is being cooperative. Then I feed my cats and tell them they're terrible and I love them. Maybe bath or nail trim for baby. Then we listen to an album while he nurses to sleep. Then I shower and brush my teeth and remind myself that brushing once a day is better than brushing zero times a day—and I probably forget I need to comb my hair.

It's nice and fulfilling, but quieter now. A circle of two, but sometimes three, or five.

My poem is almost done.

--

When we first moved the cats were good boys. Within a day or so, they would lounge about on the couches, chairs, and windowsills. There was little, if any, fighting. Unlike dogs, cats' ways are mysterious to us; that's part of their charm. They are not separated yet, but all four milling about. What's strange is that they have a whole house across two floors and a basement to spread out, but they don't. Once, in the middle of the night,

I came down for a glass of water or juice, and three of them were lined up on the sofa, one on each cushion. The Thai was missing out on the cat jamboree, but three cats together is not nothing.

A-hah, my husband and I said, *we have done it*. This means having four cats is not insane. This means moving from our house in Texas to a house in Massachusetts was the right call. This means we are functional, full adults, with our small baby we had later in life, not because we took longer to get our shit together, but because we are a careful, conscientious people.

In the middle of moving boxes around and around like a toddler moving food on their plate because they don't want to eat any of it, having cats underfoot is, of course, a hazard, but comforting to know the barriers between us and the wilderness outside are permeable, are artificial, in a way.

The house in Massachusetts sits on the precipice of woods. The trees are casually tall here, asserting themselves. We're the *them* here, in the *us and them*. I begin to learn their names: white pine, birch, American beech. When we arrive, it's the tail end of fall and I see what it's all about—a dissonant note held and held, until it's not.

--

I am looking at myself in the mirror and it's hard. It's in the same mirror my husband used as a child—a blue bathroom, full of knickknacks. It's haunted by someone else's childhood. Does the mirror think I don't belong there?

My eyes look dead, hooded, and recessed like the beginnings of churches. I have two large sleeping bags under them. My skin hasn't seen makeup for months. My skin changes colors with hormonal acne I get now. Lips split. I've been making little munching movements, a communion of self I don't have to share with others.

In the blue bathroom, a blue trash can is full of red. My period has returned. As I empty the trash can into a bag, a sense of shame comes over me. Like, after all this, I am somehow a girl again, with my girl trash. In the hamper in the bathroom closet are my stains, interrobangs, peonies, copper smell.

Now, in the thick of winter, my head begins to itch. Not constantly, but enough to where I notice it. I learn this is because my head is regrowing the hair it lost, not just the usual occasional dandruff I have to use store-brand Head and Shoulders once a week for. I look like a thumb. I could have sworn I had bones under there at one point, making a kind of shape. I was never one to know what kind of face I had, but it was certainly a shape. And now—this paper bag. Pasty. Tired. Can hair go wan? My hair is going wan. But less limpid. I compare my hair to a selfie I took a few months ago. The hair is certainly bigger now. I am regrowing as the trees are dying for the winter.

Perhaps it is a mistake to see these two as opposites, though. Both are a kind of settling in. An earth reset as I body-reset. It's hard to see my body as resetting, after growing a life, after a life was pulled from a wound.

--

I am running down the stairs, hoping no one is noticing that I smell like piss and have a suspicious dark patch on my right thigh. I have bedhead, but that's the least of my worries. Rolling in the kitchen is an orange-striped, black, and gray-striped, three-headed fur tornado, and it's headed straight for the creamsicle. There are hisses, yelling, a baby crying upstairs, and I am all fist.

All I can feel is violence and rage and a desire to hurt. All four cats know better. Only the human baby gets off the hook, and that's pushing it. I have tried gentle parenting on the cats. I have tried bribes. But I need them to know that bullying has consequences, and I am, after all, my father's daughter. I start flailing, wet thigh, sticking out bare foot. I hate being barefoot, I think—it's cold and I don't want anyone to see how much I've been picking at callouses, worse than ever. The gray-striped cat, the youngest and sort of a permanent kitten looks over his shoulder, across his enormous ass, his yellow eyes full of betrayal.

After months of getting along like cordial coworkers, the environment turns hostile. I feel like a terrible manager. Forget cat mom, I can't get them to stop fighting. It's three against one—everyone hates the creamsicle, who is a coward and was declawed by a previous owner. He is fat and lumbering and yowling. There were a few instances since we moved that we tried to write off as best we could. He peed by the food because the litter boxes were a disaster. He pooped on the floor because he got scared when we were rearranging the furniture. But you can only lie to yourselves to a point.

My husband needs help. He is standing over the bed, fully dressed, asking me to get myself up. I don't want to do it. For one thing, I'm tired. For another thing, during a midnight nursing I had somehow wet my pajama pants. I didn't want to change them because then my husband would know and I was deeply embarrassed. (Because going back to bed with urine on your clothes is somehow better?) Finally, there was some built-up resentment in being the default parent. Meaning, I knew our roles were different by virtue of him working outside the home and me being a stay-at-home parent, but it felt like I always had to handle my shit and never could catch a break. Except I'm not handling my shit—I hold it for hours on end.

The baby is fussing during television time? I go to him. The baby is fussing on the floor or rolling too far? I get down on the floor with him. The baby is spitting up? I grab a napkin. Doesn't matter that my husband is off work. I am not. I never am.

(My husband is not the villain of this piece. Time and my temper are the only villains. But time is also the solver of this problem—we talked it over, we made it better, and it's fine. Just new-parent adjustment.)

On this morning, my husband is panicked and overwhelmed because the cats are fighting. It's always the worst chaos at mealtime, which happens at 8 a.m. and 8 p.m. The 8 p.m. shift is my duty and I do it well. I take the creamsicle upstairs, even though he doesn't like to be held, and feed him separately. The other boys are calmer without him. I'm calmer without him shitting himself all over the wood floor. My husband was in a hurry, so he didn't do this, and now he needs my help.

I leave the baby in his travel crib and run downstairs in my pee pants. After the kicking and the foods and running back upstairs and crying about myself, I realize something has to change here. I don't want a house of shit and piss. I don't want a house with someone like me in it.

--

In the middle of playing with my baby with my mother-in-law and husband, my phone rings. It's on silent, so I don't hear it. When I go to look at my phone there's a missed call and a voicemail from my cousin. Well, she's not my cousin. Or, she could be. I want to protect her privacy here. This next part is about her health—it's not about me, so we have to make some concessions. Let's say cousin, but it could be a sister, a family-friend, a relation close in age whom I grew up with and with whom my parents enjoyed drawing negative parallels too. She's the good one, I'm the bad one.

In the voicemail my cousin sounds like she's in a daze, like she's someone in a play. Her lines are that something is going on with her health and I need to call her back, her thin, quiet voice thinner and quieter. So I call her back, but it goes straight to voicemail. I am thinking cancer. I am thinking she's going to die, all alone. And not in the sense that everyone dies alone, but in the sense that she never partnered, because she's a workaholic. And she's a workaholic to cover up how insecure and alone she is.

Upstairs, I pace between our bedroom and my husband's office, tracing the same figure eight in the carpet. I think about skating, how I've never been, outside of a few times in rinks in junior high, and I was always horrible, because I'm ungraceful and ungainly. I would never be brave enough for a frozen pond here.

Finally, five minutes later, my cousin calls back. I say, So, um, what's up? The first thing she says is it's not cancer, which is an excellent thing to clarify. What comes out is that she's a medical mystery. What comes out is her hair.

A month later, I unpack a picture from my wedding from a few years earlier. I'm in my old room getting ready. My cousin is a bridesmaid and the two of us are laughing. My hair is a perfect pixie (this is before I started cutting it myself), sprayed and so richly brown. It looks incapable of turning gray. But my cousin's hair is the real star here, as far as hair goes. It's her one great beauty. Thick and long. Will hold a curl if she applies rollers or a hot iron. It's a slightly lighter shade than mine. It's perfect.

And now, every time she showers it comes out. And every time she walks. And when there's a breeze. And when she moves. And when she gets dressed.

What's more alarming is that the doctors don't know why. Hair loss is bad and scary and personal, but what does it mean? If you were to Google it, you would find terrifying things like kidney disease. You would find things like autoimmune diseases, such as psoriasis.

In the coming weeks my cousin goes to specialists and then more specialized specialists. The diagnosis lands on alopecia totalis. It's all going to come out.

For now I say what I think you should say: *I'm here for you, we're going to do this one day at a time, we're going to make this okay, this sounds hard, this sounds scary, I'm so sorry.*

--

My husband mentions getting rid of the cat the morning of the breakfast disaster. The creamsicle is obviously unhappy. I say, *Fine, go outside and strangle him them, twist his neck and be done with it.* My husband is taken aback and says he meant find him a new owner, not kill him. I feel hot shame fill my cheeks.

--

Besides writing words in parentheses, there are other ways to say without saying. Umberto Eco had a great quote about this, which was to put it in quotes, attributed to someone else. You can say, "Not to sound cliché but, like they say, I'm having the time of my life." Or, "I don't mean to be rude, but I'm drowning here." Or, "I'm sorry to bother you, but I don't know how I can talk about, let alone deal with the fact that my cousin is in pain and really needs me but has been rude and dismissive to me for not having a degree and having bullshit jobs, and I don't know how to handle this." Or, "I want to be the good guy here, I think. But like the TV show about the sad horse says, there's no bad guys, there's no good guys, there's just guys." Or, "There's no script on how to accept what's happening to someone else, so we are all just doing our best here, like they say." Whoever they are. I'm sure their hair is perfect, like Warren Zevon says.

--

One cold day as fall is bleeding into winter, my husband and I go for a hike. It's a stroll, but the temperature forces us to bundle, so it feels like a hike. I wear my new Carhartt boots and new Carhartt overalls over flannel. I have a puffy green vest. My hair is buried under a slouchy yellow beany I had asked for for Christmas a few years back.

Exercise here is so much less about aesthetics than it is in Dallas. You just put on your clothes and go. It's not getting outdoors so you can get the evidence of having done so on the internet. But, regardless, I'm glad I look okay, coming into my own, in my masculine-mother fashion, hiding my distended belly and sagging breasts and disgraceful hair. It is not enough to bear children; we must erase all evidence of having done so.

Our baby is with my in-laws, so we don't have to worry about things like being out too long in the cold and if the terrain has gotten too rugged for the second-hand stroller. I think about holding hands, but I put mine in my pockets, because I still haven't gotten gloves.

The trail is largely straight. It's part of the central Massachusetts rail trail system, which means it's mostly paved. This section is elevated, so on either side is the wilderness, etcetera. Like the body, there isn't much one can say about the wilderness without thrusting one's own self into it, like seeing only your reflection floating in the glass above a scene.

The trees have a rootedness here that they don't have in Texas. A kind of casualness in size and scale. A *yes, I'm here, I'm huge, what of it?* There may very well be a few trees this size in suburban Texas, but they make such a thing of themselves that the tone is different. On either side of where we walk the trees are unyielding to scrub. They grow stalwartly as any family. They have always been there and they always will.

Between the trees, ponds pop up, marshy, slushy things, the water between fall and winter moods. Everything a cold gray, all the more beautiful for being indifferent to us two hikers. There is no wind, no birds. Just a married couple leaving footprints in their wake, in cold dirt.

As we traipse through the woods and lengthening shadows, the ponds change their character. Instead of being waded into by the trees, the trees turn to sharp points. Gothic cathedral under construction. Paralyzed gesture without force.

My husband has to point this out and I feel like a fool: beavers. They have been making their lodges here, this is their work. Between the truncated stumps are walls of logs, woven logs like fingers. They have stopped up the ponds and rerouted the water.

When we return home, I look up why beavers do that. When I was a child, I was taught that they are making their homes—which doesn't quite explain why they need to reroute the water to make a lodge. As an adult, I came to believe that the beavers simply hated the sound of running water and decided to, as a species, do something about it. The former was more accurate: they are making the water into shallow ponds to live in.

When I think of devastation, I rarely think of it as part of nature. I think of the Trinity River in Dallas, full of pollution, plastic, trash. I think of the trails by my old home, the Whataburger wrappers smearing the scrub.

My body looks like a wreckage, too, these days. The stretch marks retreating slowly, less red, but wrinkling instead. My crows feet. My breasts are at my elbows. Above my pubic hair—so unruly these days—a slice that stings sometimes, even five months later. My eyes are sort of eggy—smeary and outside of their boundaries often.

When we turn around after walking about half an hour and walk back through the chewed-up forest, all I can think about is the ecosystem. The water, disturbed. The trees, half-gone. And no doubt the animals are disturbed by this too—the fish have to go elsewhere, the birds must have to say goodbye to their nests. So much is lost in this rearranging of a home. I think that the scientists ought to do something, right? Other species live here and they matter just as much as the beavers. All I can think is the word "ecosystem," but then, as the gray light slips away into pitch black, so black you can see the stars, wait, wait: the beavers *are* the ecosystem.

--

Our own ecosystem at home needs a little rearranging. My nerves are shot. If I see one of the cats sniff a little too intently, I see a cat jump too high, my instincts go into overdrive. I leap up and make sure they're not voiding their bowels or spraying. I'm on edge. I'm sick of being angry and upset at wild animals trying to make a new house work for them. So, after moving furniture around in the basement, we stick the creamsicle in it. That's his new home. It's unfortunate because he was always the victim, but it doesn't make sense to have three cats trapped in the basement, even though the three of them are bullies to the creamsicle.

We go down to the basement to play with him. We feed him. He gets even fatter. He sits at the top of the wooden stairs and sobs to get out.

But there's no shit on the floors, no piss on the carpets. The other three seem more relaxed, even friendly. They take a few days to forget what I did, with my kicking feet, with my yelling voice, which makes me feel like maybe I was too harsh on myself for losing my temper at them, which makes me feel worse.

--

With my cousin's permission, I ask for help online. I have social media, she doesn't. On a filtered post, I write:

Hello friends, I need some assistance. Any advice would be appreciated.

TL;DR: Someone close to me is going through health stuff and could use some support.

Let's call her Q. She's mid-thirties. Unpartnered. Lives alone. (Not to make it sound like she's a shut-in. She's fun and funny and smart! She is a career-first kind of type A! Just to give context!)

Here are the ways she could use support:

    A. Physical

        B. Mental / Emotional

        C. [Editing this in] Sleep

A. Physical. So I'm going to keep health stuff a little vague in the name of privacy. But she had something super weird happen where her hair fell out. Like, half of it. There is a physical cause that is being addressed. (It's not super threatening like cancer or COVID.) Her scalp is super sensitive, so some stuff like a rough wool beanie may be right out. What can she do right now? Any cancer survivors or COVID long-haulers here? What worked or didn't? Idk? A good scarf? A good wig?

She has a job facing people, like a car saleswoman or professor or doctor, so her appearance is a thing. And even if her job were solitary spelunking, hair is a big, big deal. It's not silly or vain to be upset about dramatic physical changes brought on by illness! I was unmoored by my postpartum hair loss, and it was super minor compared to this!

Hair is (was) long, straight, and thick, and a single-layer cut.

B. Mental / emotional. I know when I was going through stuff with my C-section and weird vomit reaction to lactation, I had physical and emotional support in a way Q simply doesn't. I know things like Uber Eats and subscriptions to HBO and Spotify ruled. I can take care of those for Q. But is there something I'm missing? Like, um, a good therapeutic thing? Or??? What can I do to be there for Q during this time? I picked a hecking time to move from Texas!

Q is going to have this thing and hair loss up to two years. People with chronic conditions, what keeps you sane?

C. Sleep issues. Due to the medication she's on, she's having chronic sleep issues. I'm sure the anxiety isn't helping. Like, we all know obvious stuff like teas, melatonin (although idk how that plays off meds), white noise machine, etc. But what is something we may not be thinking of? Like something that works for you that's off the wall, like you rub an orange on your brow and cross your eyes and eat a brownie? Speaking of which, I don't think Q would be open to CBD or w33d.

Texas friends, in a Q-emergency is driving about an hour out of DFW north a thing you can do? You don't know Q but you know me. Think of this as me calling in a favor and then owing you several. (This part is a plan B—like having a list of people I can call upon in a pinch—if it comes to that. Obvi I'm going to fly out but like I have a baby and live on the other side of the country, so it's good to have a contingency plan or several.)

Oh! Important edit: Q doesn't do social media. Which under normal circumstances I would say is a good choice for mental health ...

And people rallied. If there's one thing I'm good at, it's rallying people to a cause. My backyard DIY wedding another good example of this—so many people helping, out of kindness and the good feeling that comes with being useful. I got advice about sleep podcasts, wigs, hats, scarves, silk pillowcases, finding a therapist, people volunteering to be a contact person if Q needs something. It was truly amazing. If you're ever feeling lonely, asking for help and favor is a good route. I forget this.

I email the responses I get to Q in three emails: An Email About Hair, An Email about Wellness (ew), and An Email about Sleep. Emails don't have an urgency to them the way texting does and I don't need a reply. Q texts to say she got the email when I send something as I think of it.

--

As the days get shorter, they take on a new shape. The last gasp of fall is a still time. Most of the leaves are already fallen and have become the forest floor. It is not a time of arriving. It is not a time of being a new person—it's preparing for that. It's an almost, but not yet.

Here are what most days are like:

I'm sad and scared and tired. But I'm putting on the most chipper, brave face I can because, for whatever reason, I found myself in the role of long-distance caretaker.

Well, not for whatever reason. We are related. But also, it just feels heavy and odd that people go, "Ah, yes, the most sarcastic, dead-pan, abrasive bitch around. Must be nurturing. Let's go." But I can do it: I'm pragmatic and compassionate and organized. But I can't.

My cousin in Texas is a medical mystery. She's not okay. I'm not okay either. Obviously her problems aren't my problems, but I think I get to say I'm not okay either.

I'm here in Massachusetts with a baby. I'm here in a new place, with no friends physically near me, trying to build a life for myself, but having a baby, and making friends as an adult is hard.

So I make sure Q eats, buy her stuff she needs or doesn't, email her stuff about her conditions and how not to go lose her mind when shit is hitting the fan, and then call her every day and we watch the new *She-Ra*. Her for the first time, me for the third. I say, *Oh no, I'm getting an echo. Let's pause. I'm at 8 minutes 2 seconds. Get to that spot then we'll do 1, 2, 3 go, but then I'll wait a second because my TV response time is faster than yours.*

We do that for an hour or so. And I try to just let this be what it is and not think about how we're both alone in different ways and our work looks so different from each other's. I don't teach at a university or have a job respected by society, but this is work, too. I try to let this be what it is and not think about how she was always the golden child, with a slim waist and beautiful, perfect, thick hair, and I tend to fatten, and my hair is thin and frizzy, and these physical differences were one of the ways in which our parents made her the good one and me the bad one. But really that's only the start. I try not to think in categories like "golden child" and "scapegoat" and "black sheep," because I'm not a sheep or a goat, and why the fuck would anybody want me to take care of them? Besides a baby who has no choice and doesn't know any better.

Wait, no, now you're ahead. Pause for a second while I catch up.

And it sucks, but since it's happening to someone else, you don't want to be like *but me* too much because that's honestly not a good look.

So most days, you wake up at five for baby and you can usually convince him to go back to sleep after you nurse him. And then you wake up for real around eight. And then it's breakfast while he rolls around, so fast and strong now. Then you make coffee and sit on the floor with him and play Panda and rattle and ball. Then he sleeps while you work on your literary magazine and check for rejections—you've been getting a lot lately. Then it's time for nursing and walking around the house saying *on, off* to light switches. Then it's time for emailing your cousin stuff about things. Then it's time for your lunch and sticking baby in a high chair so he gets used to people food. Then you play a silly game of *where is mommy* and read him a book. Then he naps and you read and draw and write something that'll get rejected soon. Then you nurse him and call your sister and watch TV. Then you do laundry, but you left a tissue in the pocket of your overalls, and for whatever reason, that's the thing that makes you cry, just big, ugly tears, at your wet piles of laundry, covered in tissue debris because, fuck, you fucked up. But you just put it in the dryer anyway and decide to deal with it later. Then it's time for cleaning and unpacking and then dinner and maybe *Jeopardy!* and introducing solid food and nursing with an album to sleep and then showering and probably forgetting to comb your damn hair. But at least you still have it. Be grateful. Be grateful.

--

In the months since we've moved to New England, I've only written one poem, and *The Book of Matches* literary magazine was kind enough to publish it in their Spring 2023 issue. It's about that end of fall feeling, about how we can never view nature but through the lens of self, as captured in the final image.

That or I just wanted to write about cat anuses.

This is a tangent, but I wanted to give a sense of where I am as my cousin's hair falls out, how all around me is shedding. In me too, as my uterine lining slides out between my legs.

Cider

After four weeks, I had seen enough,
like knowing someone from how they treat a waiter.
O, I want to infuse this poem with light
like inserting lemon jelly into a donut, but around
these parts, what you get are apple cider donuts,
which are a marriage of earth and air,
like cracked lips in the cold. The twiggiest
of treats, red like a heart in a jar, sugar crunch,
puckered like a cat's anus,
stained glass in the cathedral of mouth.

*

Here, the cats are not merely decorous and indolent,
but useful in being near. At night,
one black like that space between stars
and one striped like birch find their way
in valleys of bodies and blankets,
immobile and warm as rocks. Greek chorus
with the oil heater clicking through the baseboards.
Four yellow candles. It's enough for the room.

*

The white pines buttress sky,
which is whirled with clouds like marble.
The old railroads turned aisle by gravel.
Here, it is always late afternoon, cusping
evening. Vespers for those who observe,
pilgrims who've come such a long, long way.
Donation box, no candles, God's own pay phone.
Meanwhile, the American beech has gone monstrance gold.
Meanwhile, the birds have departed.
Meanwhile, lichen signal beginning of ordinary time
for the rock, the birch. But even so,
one twig turned reptile in orange vestments.

*

For the last of the day, I nurse my son
with the lamp only, and I stare
across the unmade bed—flannel like afterbirth,
red and puddly. Below my window,
the trees are incandescent with death,
but I cannot see them. Out in the black,
between the stars, my reflection.
Ensconced in an old hoodie, bunched to the upper third
of my torso, leggings, hair gone twig.
Pink head at my breast, we're floating
with our doubles in the glass. I wiggle a bit,
but I cannot be untwinned. I know now
I have seen only as if coming out of a thick sleep.

--

I was the one that helped the cat at our old house. I covered for him. My son was still nursing at night at that age. I hadn't mastered nursing in bed yet—something about the geometry of breasts and a baby's head. I couldn't get it to work. I would go out into the living room and nurse on an old red chair, my feet on a plastic stool for children from Ikea. Then I would put the baby back to sleep in the bassinet in the bedroom and go back out to the kitchen while my husband slept and look for cat pee. Always there was some pee. A little piss over by the back door, sinking into the floor which was rotting anyways. Before my husband would notice in the morning, I would go and clean up the puddle and not tell him. My fear was that he would take the creamsicle away. It wasn't that he would actually do this; it was that my abandonment issues run deep. The fear that anyone or anything I had ever loved would be taken away.

My C-section was unplanned. My son had wrapped his cord around his neck and was choking himself with each contraction. I thought we're losing him, but I thought it like a robot would. I just assume everything I love will be taken away.

I saw a meme in one of the various therapy groups I'm in that was like: "Are you a push-everyone-away-so-they-don't-leave-you anxious person or a get-overly-clingy anxious person?" and I realized I was both.

That's why I said what I said about just killing the creamsicle. Get it over with. My husband loves the cat too and would never. I just wanted to have some control.

After I nursed my son at night, I would see huge puddles and be surprised I didn't smell anything. My nose must have gone numb. Embarrassing to think guests could smell your house when you assumed it was fine. Not that we were having many guests. I didn't like to clean in my bare feet but going back to the bedroom for shoes seemed like too much fuss and might wake the baby. So it was crouching as far apart and as low as the C-section would let me with paper towels, spray, wait, and then more paper towels. I would put the paper towels in a plastic bag and toss into the garage with the rest of the trash and never mention this to my husband.

They are good cats. They get to stay. The creamsicle didn't mean it.

When I couldn't smell, I could still taste as I was cleaning up the piss. I'd wear a mask if I found one easily, fumbling around in the dull kitchen light, the outside musty with light pollution. But mask or not, the pepper taste of spray. Or was that the piss? The two are permanently linked for me. Pepper and lemon from a tree that grows in hell.

--

I post on my Facebook, filtered audience:

It's been a long two days. Q's issues continue to be mysterious, but it's looking like it may be autoimmune. I'm sleepless. Which is funny because my son is sleeping like an angel, so the person keeping me awake is me.

Q is actually a family member. I'm keeping her anonymous for her privacy—although given how few people I talk to from my family of origin, it doesn't take a genius to work out. I'm including that detail because I'm trying to make clear the gravity and feelings at play. Not that you can't be very invested in the well-being of a friend or family of choice, of course! It just hits different.

If nothing else, we've known each other our whole lives and have a unique, shared language.

Anyways, I'm grateful for the outpouring of support and suggestions and have been passing them along via email. There's something less urgent about an email vs text, which is why I've been doing it that way.

I realized something as I was trying to get some rest. I asked for suggestions from people with chronic conditions, and the more voices we have, the better and stronger we all are. But I was asking in such a way that I was marking myself not in that group. Isn't that funny? That I "othered" a group of people despite having two debilitating conditions. Is it because I have internalized ableism (probably)? Or because I feel like an imposter with my issues because they're not "bad enough" and "don't count" because patriarchy? (Yeah.) It's wild to be like "I have no idea what chronic issues are like halp," and also, "I sometimes scream until I pass out when I'm on my period," and "My bladder is goofy because it's covered in uterine tissue oops." Weird, right? Again, I'm so glad I asked, and I'm infinitely grateful for your input, but I should have asked myself, too.

I'm so tired right now.

--

I buy my husband and myself things on Amazon when I'm bored and want to pretend my hair is my worst trait. I buy a detangling brush. My husband brushes his curls until he looks like Beethoven. I like the way the brush feels on my scalp, which is itchy with new growth. I buy dry shampoo because showering isn't a thing I can do every day anymore. (Q says she stopped cleaning herself because her hair comes out in the shower.) I buy a book called the *Curly Girl Method*. I hate it. It's confusing. It starts with here are the types of curls, which one are you? Here are two models with S waves. And the models' hair look nothing like each other. I buy microfiber towels for tearing.

I buy my cousin things too. Coloring books for when she's sad. Silk pillowcases. Groceries.

--

Something I left out in talking about my new digs was that we moved in with my in-laws. It didn't seem important to what I was trying to say and I didn't want the assumptions about moving back in with your parents. It's not like that. It is like that. But it does seem mentioning relative to my feeling not at home. It's hard to feel at home in someone else's childhood bedroom. It's not my house. I just live here. Same with my body.

My mother-in-law intermingles our chairs with theirs. We have cheap Ikea furniture that we spay-painted. A red chair, a forest green chair, a turquoise chair, and a yellow, which was my husband's concession to me wanting everything yellow. My in-laws' chairs have a wicker bottom and dark wood backs. I am not one to know trees, even when they're dead. The six chairs for the four of us look pretty good mixed in together.

The plan was for us to use the money from our house in Texas to build an addition for them. It's been months and we haven't started. It's hard to expand as we all grow smaller in our various ways.

--

My cousin becomes too much to keep up with, in a way. She's on winter break from her job as a professor and has too much time to think about her situation. She doesn't have to say it, but she doesn't think of my job as a job. As a way of being compassionate to both of us, I suggest a routine. I call her every day at three o'clock my time and we watch an episode or two of *She-Ra and the Princesses of Power*. It's a cartoon for children, which I've already seen twice. I wanted something I didn't have to pay too much attention to.

In the reboot of the show from the '80s, the hero, Adora, learns she was on the wrong side of the war and learns she is the latest reincarnation of a superhero, She-Ra. She teams up with princesses and fights. The opening song is a giveaway: We're going to win in the end.

It's funny and zany and heart-warming and positive but also deals with trauma and mommy-issues.

The first time I watched the show with my husband he remarked that one of the princesses, Entrapta, sounds just like my cousin, but more honky. My cousin does not have a Midwest, flat-voweled accent. I didn't hear it at first, but he's right. The cadence and excitable bursts are the same. Entrapta hyperfocuses on science, my cousin on the subject she teaches at the small university in Texas. They both believe in the supremacy of their special interests and don't much care how anyone else feels about them.

In the words of Entrapta: Science!

I tell my cousin this, and she's not as amused as I am. What I don't tell her is the irony or aptness—you choose—of Entrapta not having hair either. Instead she has long, pink tentacles which are more akin to that of an octopus, without the suctions, than hair. Entrapta's hair is magical and like limbs she can walk on. No one makes a thing out of Entrapta not having any hair; that's just how some people are. The other characters are not accepting of her appearance because there is nothing to accept. Hair, tentacles, it doesn't matter, in a world of bright colors, capers, and friendship where trauma lasts a few seasons instead of a lifetime.

--

Another way of saying without saying is to go on diversions with facts that resonate. You can make the reader draw their own conclusions. This only looks like artistry.

For example, did you know researchers have been studying eel reproduction with great puzzlement for some time now? The how and the why of eel reproduction seem like different questions. And all of it is terrifying. I read online that eels go, instinctively, to the Sargasso Sea and then spawn and die. Sometimes they go over land. All they need is a dampness. Drawn like a needle on a compass to the spawning ground. Once they slither-swim there, they fuck and then die. Seeing as they die before raising their young, how does the next generation know?

What's also odd is researchers have yet to find any reproductive organs, so a lot is conjecture. An article said that scientists have made a lot of headway on the issue of eels fucking, but a good deal remains a mystery. Eels have been around for a while, so I find that remarkable—have made a lot of headway. The article begins with a description of eels; it is not simply a snake fish. It must have fins in specific places, and it must produce slime. Some live in freshwater, some live in saltwater, but all fuck in saltwater regardless.

Juvenile eels do not have genitals but develop them sometime, somehow. Secret changes, secret becoming. It's really none of our business, when you think about it. The eels slime themselves over dry land to the Sargasso Sea. Fuck somehow, then die. But it's like with sea turtles: since their parents were already dead by the time they came of age, how did they know where to go, what to do?

Instinctual codes for keeping safe. Instinctual codes, all the little eels, having them. Does the knowledge come with genitals? Does the blossoming eel say, *Ah-ah, I have it, I know what it's for and what I must do?*

--

Here is another story: a soldier from WWI, Sargent Thomas Kitching, was shot in the thigh. When his thigh was amputated, he fashioned the bone into a brooch and gave it to his girlfriend. The bone is now in a museum. The museum's website states little is known about the piece of macabre jewelry, but I think we know enough.

It's like holy communion and wood combined. Which, makes sense—it's what we are, wood and bread, divine and of the earth. It has cracks running through the yellow-white, peaks and valleys, set in a silver curling frame. The broach is now in an exhibition on WWI at University of Leeds. Although I don't think this has much to do with WWI, besides it coming from a soldier's thigh bone.

Is there not beauty here, too? Is there not a statement to be made about art and human suffering?

What did the girlfriend think of the brooch? The museum does not speculate. I like to think she thought it was sweet. Not a piece of his heart, but a piece. A literal object. Can you imagine? (I carry it in my heart, I carry it with me.) Where did she pin it? By her neck, maybe? On her scarf? What did she tell people? *Oh what an unusual brooch! Thank you—it's a piece of my boyfriend. His bone.*

--

In an online shopping splurge to cure my depression, I buy a detangling brush TikTok is apparently wild about. It's under $15 and makes my scalp feel nice. My husband likes it too. It's pink-handled and friendly, the spokes reaching out like black fingers. Most importantly, it works. Just because something is gentle doesn't mean it doesn't work. All of my tangles smoothed down like butter, hair going liquid, something making me worthy of touch. I say without thinking about it: "I wish I had this as a kid, then I wouldn't have gotten in trouble because of my hair."

My husband is puzzled and asks, "Why did you get in trouble because of your hair? It's just hair."

Once a week my father used to brush all of our hair before church. Mine was a disaster, always, But even at five, I knew it was unfair: who had hair that could stay neat a whole week?

Q did. The first girl allowed to grow her hair past her jawbone. Long and thick and perfect.

My father was in charge of our haircuts. And bath time.

Everyone said how beautiful her hair was. Thick, pin-straight, never a bother. She never needed much for it—which is how you knew she was good. She never needed creams or special shampoos. A simple $3 brush from Target. I still remember it—it had a blue handle.

My father is pulling my hair--rats' nest--he is seething. Rats' nest.

Sometimes when I get a tangle and I don't have detangler, I put my conditioner on a comb and glide it through the back of my head slowly, until it undoes itself.

My father starts at the top, by the child-scalp, already flaking from not enough care, yanks the brush through wild growth that ended in a blunt bob. It was never enough. When we went to the hairdresser, they had a hard time with it too, and would yank and pull. Cutting my bangs, one hairdresser said I had a widow's peak, I didn't know I had death on my face until someone told me. I thought it made my face shaped like a heart.

At age thirty-two, I finally learn the correct way to brush my hair is by starting at the ends and then getting to the roots, that way you're not ripping on your way down.

Gentle things can work too.

--

On the third watch of *She-Ra*, I am struck by the awful truth that Entrapta gets left behind. I hate that I drew the comparison to Q, because at this point, I don't know what is going to happen. On the white couch that my in-laws complain about but my husband and I find adequate, I have my phone pressed to my ear with Q and my eyes on the TV. My infant is watching too, from his gray and white swing, but it's a cartoon, so it doesn't count as television for him. It's a baby looking at art.

On the show a rescue mission goes awry and Entrapta is abandoned in the enemy camp. The other princesses are devastated and think she's dead. They sit under the weight of their own failure, their own inadequacy.

It's hard to focus on the show with the phone, the baby, my in-laws in the kitchen and other parts of the house. So I don't. Q is here but she's not.

Both of us are left behind.

--

Bleeding winter, I go. My hair is buried.

My mother, my distended belly and breasts and hair. It is not enough to bear; we must erase all evidence of having done so.

My baby worry the terrain has gotten too rugged. I think about holding.

the wilderness, etcetera. thrusting one's own self into it.

rootedness here. size and scale. yes, I'm here, I'm huge, what of it? unyielding to scrub. They grow stalwartly as any family. They have always been there, and they always will.

Everything a cold gray, all the more beautiful for being indifferent.

shadows turn to sharp points.

I feel like a wall, woven logs like fingers. They rerouted the water.

home, When I was a child, I remember being taught that they are making their homes—hated the sound.

When I think of devastation, I think of it as part of nature. I think of the Trinity River in Dallas, full of pollution, plastic, trash. I think of the trails by my old home, the Whataburger wrappers smearing the scrub.

My body looks like a wreckage, too, these days. The stretch marks retreating slowly, less red, but wrinkling instead. My crows feet. My breasts are at my elbows. Above my pubic hair—so unruly these days—a slice that stings sometimes, even eight months later outside of boundaries.

Disturbed. Half-gone. the animals are disturbed by this too. So much is lost in this rearranging of a home. I ought to do something, live here and matter.

--

After two weeks of talking to Q for an hour five days a week, we stop. She gets busy going back to work. She forgets to text me about updates, like going to the doctor. But we did so much more than talk about her hair and watch TV—and I think she wants to forget this. The whole ordeal brought us closer together, and now we're both a little embarrassed.

We talked about hair loss, about therapy, about our roles in the family, and how unfair it all was. I say looking at my son, *Sometimes all I can think about is how can you look at a baby and not tell them you love them? Not even once? How can you not kiss their little face, wipe their tears? How can you not?*

But in that pocket of time, which exists in telephone signals and Wi-Fi and Netflix being watched in sync, at the tail end of Christmas break, I am working quietly. Making sure Q eats by asking, *What did you eat today?* and letting her know that things like a handful of meat and a handful of shredded cheese do in fact count. When just trying to survive, all kinds of things count. I don't say this, but I know what counts, about taking half-measures, due to the bought of depression in my twenties. Can't do dishes? That's fine. Just get the ones out of your bed. Can't take a shower? Also fine. Can you wash your face? Things like that. That's how I got by. You can get by this way for years.

--

One night I can't sleep and I stumble around Wikipedia for a while. The person who keeps me awake the most is me. Next to my husband who is asleep and not snoring, I beam a stream of bright information directly into my eyeballs.

I read about Pandanus language. In New Guinea several native groups have adopted an avoidance language when gathering karuka nuts. The idea is that words in their native tongues are harmful to the plants. If the plants hear the wrong words, they won't grow like they're supposed to. The nut-gatherers, at harvest time, employ a Pandanus language, a vocabulary of about a thousand words or so. It is only used when gathering karukas, lest the mountain spirits overhear and come down to investigate.

I want to believe that it works. If you use the right words, the harvest will go well.

--

In an online moms' group, a mother posts that she doesn't know what to do about her six-year-old daughter. The daughter gets excited about her baby tooth wiggling and says she's looking forward to the tooth fairy. After worrying it back and forth for a day, she gently pries it out. The blood spurts down her child face and she cries immediately. The mother makes sure she isn't hurt and asks, *What is it, what is it?* All the child can manage to say is, *I wasn't ready.* It does not matter that the new tooth is already asserting itself. It doesn't matter that just moments ago the child was excited for this shedding. All that matters is she knows she can't regrow the same tooth twice.

--

A woman with graying hair in a home haircut sits at the top of the basement steps. The door to the kitchen is shut behind her and there's just enough room on the landing for her enormous ass. She pats both of her knees to coax the creamsicle up the stairs to where she is sitting. The creamsicle is surprisingly lithe for a cat built like a bulldog and comes bounding up, yowling the whole time. He plops into the woman's lap, getting his orange fur all over her stretched-out leggings. She pats the cat, face to rump, face to rump. "(I love you)," she says, and "(babydoll)," and "(I am so sorry)."

Notes on Poems

"Grendel's Mother Considers Vinegar" alludes to Toni Morrison's essay "Grendel and His Mother" in its first and final lines: "Evil has no father." Morrison's essay can be found in her posthumous collection *The Source of Self-Regard: Selected Essays, Speeches, and Meditations*, published by Knopf, 2019.

"Hole Shapes" is after "Watching My Friend Pretend Her Heart Is Not Breaking" by Rosemerry Wahtola Trommer

Notes on Poems

Acknowledgments

Grateful acknowledgement is given to the following:

To *Pink Panther* for publishing "In Defense of Gentleness" and "Painting by Mary Cassatt" (Fall 2023).

To *Jarfly* for publishing "Snapshots for My Family" (Fall 2022).

To *Lothlorien Review* for publishing "Hole Shapes" and Watching Perry Mason with a Mouth Full of Vomit" (Summer 2022).

To *Agapanthus Collective* for publishing "Red Sea Whale" (Spring 2023).

To *Banyan Review* for publishing "Teaching My Son Poetry" (Spring 2023).

To *Ocotillo Review* for publishing "Grendel's Mother Considers Wells Beach, Maine," "Grendel's Mother Considers the Sphinx Moth," and "Grendel's Mother Considers the Bones You Cannot Touch" (Winter 2023).

To *Cul-De-Sac of Blood* for publishing "Grendel's Mother Considers Ants" (Spring 2024).

To *Amethyst Review* for publishing "Grendel's Mother Considers the Surinam Toad" (Summer 2023).

To *1-70 Review* for publishing "Grendel's Mother Considers Ortolans" and "Grendel's Mother Considers Pigs" (Fall 2024).

To *Saltbush Review* for publishing "Grendel's Mother Considers Therapy" (Winter 2023).

To *Sacramento Review* for publishing "Grendel's Mother Considers the Giraffes" and "Grendel's Mother Considers the Pink Fairy Armadillo" (Winter 2023).

To *Another New Calligraphy* for publishing "Grendel's Mother Considers Convalescing" (Winter 2023).

To *Tokyo Review* for publishing "Grendel's Mother Considers Eve" (Fall 2023).

To *Quail Bell* for publishing "Grendel's Mother Considers Vinegar" and "Grendel's Mother Considers Christ the Starfish" (Fall 2023).

To *Mom Egg Review* for publishing "Grendel's Mother Considers Sea Turtles" (Spring 2024).

To *Bosphorus Review of Books* for publishing "(Hair / Loss)" (Fall 2023).

To *The Book of Matches* for publishing "Cider" (Spring 2023).

Title Index

G

Grendel's Mother Considers Ants 33
Grendel's Mother Considers Christ the Starfish 40
Grendel's Mother Considers Convalescing 35
Grendel's Mother Considers Eve 38
Grendel's Mother Considers Ortolans 24
Grendel's Mother Considers Pigs 31
Grendel's Mother Considers the Bones You Cannot Touch ...32
Grendel's Mother Considers the Giraffes 34
Grendel's Mother Considers
    the Pink Fairy Armadillo 37
Grendel's Mother Considers Therapy 25
Grendel's Mother Considers the Sea Turtles 41
Grendel's Mother Considers the Sphinx Moth 29
Grendel's Mother Considers the Surinam Toad 23
Grendel's Mother Considers Vinegar 39
Grendel's Mother Considers Wells Beach, Maine 22

H

(Hair / Loss) 44
Hole Shapes 14

I
In Defense of Gentleness 10
P
Painting by Mary Cassatt 13
R
Red Sea Whale 18
S
Snapshots for My Family 11
T
Teaching My Son Poetry 20
W
Watching Perry Mason with a Mouth Full of Vomit 16

First Line Index

A
A strange man is at my house when it is not yet light 44
B
but not as an alternative to revenge. More of a *yes* 25
C
Celestial Star, yours is the same as of the sea 40
F
Fatherless as Grendel, the vinegar has not been generated 39
H
How do you manage it—slow 24
I
I am all camera—I 11
I am trying to find a story in which an
  animal is written about fairly 29
Imagine that, not wanting or needing a name. Each 22
im sorry 38
in a sanatorium or a jail cell. It doesn't
  much matter which. But 35
in the room of given light 32

I teach 10
It's okay to be tender. Here 13
K
Kitten, I read to my son 20
M
My son has a mouth 18
N
Nobody knows how you do it. Other beasts 34
O
O small beast with little hooves 31
T
The way to carry is to care 33
W
We call my grandmother as she is dying 16
Wet webs blanket the grass in mornings 14
Y
You are fast but frigid. You forget the sounds 41
Your armor is pathetic—O my sashimi, my sand-snake 37
Your brats are bursting, big with love 23

www.ingramcontent.com/pod-product-compliance
Lightning Source LLC
Chambersburg PA
CBHW010046090426
42735CB00020B/3412